Owlways Together

A Heartwarming Poem About Love and Dreams

Raphaela Kauth

This book belongs to:

_____

A golden heart and a mind so rare,
You, our child, are beyond compare.

Watching you blossom is such a pleasure,
You are our reflection, our little treasure.

Your bright eyes, full of dreams and aspirations,
Unveil a future without any limitations.

Your ideas and dreams are incredibly unique,
A treasure of hopes and possibilities they seek.

We'll share any burden that you may bore,
Remember it isn't the end, there's always more.

Never stop trying, you'll find your way,
Your calling in life will come one day.

Don't doubt yourself, you're capable and wise,
With courage and belief, you'll reach new highs.

It often takes patience, like a slow, steady song,
But your perseverance will make you strong.

Sometimes the sun shines and sometimes it might rain,
Bringing joy or sorrow, it's nature's refrain.

We laugh at your jokes, we believe in your superpower,
Through thick and thin, we stand by you, hour by hour.

An astronaut, a firefighter, or a unicorn you can be,
Reach for the stars, and set your spirit free.

In every step you take, you leave footprints of faith,
Embrace the journey and leave a lasting trace.

The journey may have ups and downs, twists and bends,
But remember dear one, you have true friends.

With love as your compass, and dreams as your guide,
You'll conquer the world, standing tall with pride.

Dream big and bold, let your passion ignite,
Embrace possibilities, like a star twinkling bright.

So, believe in yourself, you have what it takes,
To make a difference, whatever path life makes.

With all your heart create a world of your own,
Remember, dear one, you're never alone.

Made in the USA
Las Vegas, NV
09 December 2023

82427394R00024